RECORD-BREAKING BUGS
SUPER SPIDERS

60000402279

Thanks to the creative team:

Senior Editor: Alice Peebles

Fact checking: Kate Mitchell

Designer: www.collaborate.agency

First published in Great Britain in 2016
by Hungry Tomato Ltd

PO Box 181

Edenbridge

Kent, TN8 9DP

Copyright © 2016 Hungry Tomato Ltd

No part of this publication may be reproduced,
stored in a retrieval system, or transmitted in any
form or by any means, electronic, mechanical,
photocopying, recording, or otherwise, without
the prior written permission of the
copyright owner.

A CIP catalogue record for this book is available
from the British Library.

ISBN 978-1-910684-65-8

Printed and bound in China

Discover more at
www.hungrytomato.com

Northamptonshire Libraries & Information Service BH	
Askews & Holts	

Record-Breaking Bugs
SUPER SPIDERS

by Matt Turner

Illustrated by Santiago Calle

HUNGRY
TOMATO™

CONTENTS

SPECTACULAR SPIDERS

For many of us, spiders are fearsome creatures. But they're also fascinating. They've lived on Earth for more than 300 million years, and have evolved to live in almost every dry-land habitat, from deep caves to deserts and rainforests. Many seem quite at home in our houses. Today there are more than 50,000 species of all shapes and sizes, found worldwide except Antarctica.

Spiders are not related to insects; they have eight (not six) legs, their body is in two (not three) parts, and they lack antennae. Like insects, however, spiders are arthropods. They have an exoskeleton (outer armour), which must be moulted regularly as the young spider grows to adulthood. (You can sometimes find the empty moults in their webs.) All spiders make silk, a strong thread that is spun from the spinnerets – tiny nozzles at the tip of the abdomen. Most spider species have eight eyes, but some have six, or four, or even just two.

A spider's body has two main parts: the cephalothorax (supporting the eyes, mouthparts and legs); and the abdomen (containing most of the internal organs).

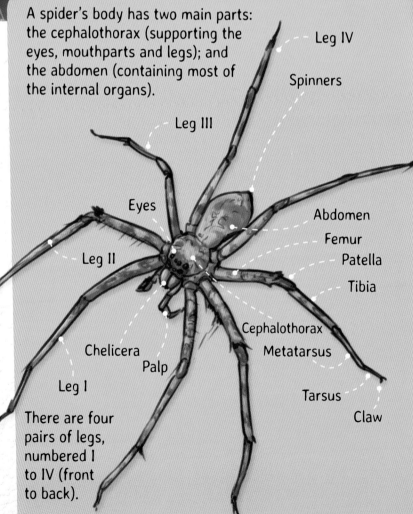

Leg IV
Spinners
Leg III
Eyes
Abdomen
Femur
Patella
Tibia
Leg II
Cephalothorax
Metatarsus
Chelicera
Palp
Tarsus
Leg I
Claw

There are four pairs of legs, numbered I to IV (front to back).

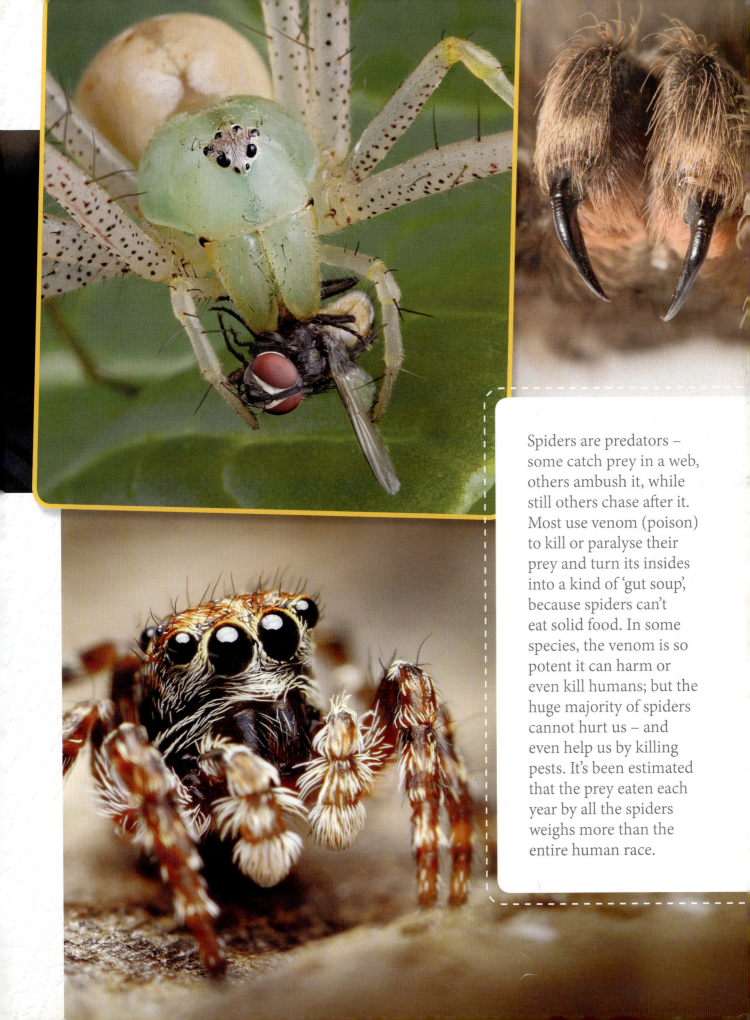

Spiders are predators – some catch prey in a web, others ambush it, while still others chase after it. Most use venom (poison) to kill or paralyse their prey and turn its insides into a kind of 'gut soup', because spiders can't eat solid food. In some species, the venom is so potent it can harm or even kill humans; but the huge majority of spiders cannot hurt us – and even help us by killing pests. It's been estimated that the prey eaten each year by all the spiders weighs more than the entire human race.

SILK & ORB WEBS

Some spiders have a *cribellum* – a rack of extra spinnerets – which spins a fine silk that is then combed by the legs to make 'woolly' silk for snaring prey.

Silk is stretchy and strong, and spiders often spin a 'dragline' when they leap or drop from a perch – such as a twig – to catch their fall.

Silk is so strong that, in earlier times, tribes in New Guinea wove it over wooden hoop-nets to catch fish from rivers.

A textile artist collected gold-coloured silk from more than a million orb weavers to make this beautiful cape.

Stabilimenta are silken zigzags that some spiders weave into their webs. Do these eye-catching designs help attract insect prey by reflecting ultraviolet light, or do they keep birds away by making the web more visible? Or do they help to make the spider look bigger? Experts aren't quite sure.

MAKING SILK

Stored as a liquid, spider silk dries into a thread after being squeezed out of the spinnerets. Spiders can spin different kinds of silk: sticky for trapping prey, non-sticky for walking on, extra-strong for hanging from, and so on. Their most famous creation is the beautiful, spiralling orb web, but many spiders build more messy-looking, three-dimensional 'tangle webs'.

GOLDEN ORB WEB SPIDER
NEPHILA CLAVIPES
Body size: female up to 50 mm (2 in);
male 5–8 mm (0.25–0.3 in)
Where found: North, Central
and South America

STRONG STUFF
Spider silk is five times stronger than steel of the same thickness. One day, it may be used to make bullet-proof vests for soldiers.

GARDEN SPIDERS
A garden spider may use up to 60 m (196 ft) of silk in a typical orb web, but usually finishes the task within an hour.

TUNNELS & TRAPDOORS

A burrowing spider uses spines on its fangs to dig a hole in the soil. It then waterproofs the burrow walls with layers of mud and spit and then silk.

A trapdoor spider adds a hinged door made of silk, mud and grasses. This hides the spider as it sits in wait for prey to wander near.

With its door shut, the burrow is hidden from view. But spider-hunting wasps can usually spot the entrance. The door is no proof against floods, either.

Spiders in the family Agelenidae, which build sheet webs above ground, add funnel-like hideaways to their webs, from which they rush out to grab prey.

The trapdoor spider Cyclosmia has a flat-ended abdomen covered with a tough plate. It uses this to 'stopper' itself inside its burrow, if threatened.

WEB TRAPS

Ancient spiders lived in holes in the ground. Some spiders still live like this today, particularly the primitive species known as *mygalomorphs*. Trapdoor spiders often add hinged lids to hide their entrance. Funnel-web spiders, by contrast, ring their entrances with silken 'trip wires' that alert them when prey is walking nearby. Above the ground, some spiders add protective tunnels of silk to their webs.

BANDED TUNNEL WEB SPIDER
HEXATHELE HOCHSTETTERI
Body size: up to 20 mm (0.78 in)
Where found: New Zealand

SUPER STRONG
Using its barbs and fangs to hold its trapdoor closed, the California trapdoor spider *Bothriocyrtum californicum* can resist a record-breaking pull of up to 38 times its own weight.

MASTER DIGGERS
Trapdoor spiders can dig tunnels 30–40 cm (12–15 in) deep in the ground, and live up to 30 years.

Venom & Hunting

Spiders' fangs work in one of two ways. The fangs on mygalomorphs (suborder Orthognatha) work up and down together, a bit like a pair of pickaxes...

...whereas in the so-called 'true' spiders (suborder Labidognatha), the fangs open and close in a side-to-side pincer action.

Trapdoor spiders are sit-and-wait predators. When prey walks near, they burst out and grab it, then pull it back into their lair.

When an insect blunders into an orb web, it takes only 5–10 seconds for the spider to rush out and bite it. Then it wraps the prey in silk before eating it.

Jumping spiders (family Salticidae) pounce on their prey like tigers. There are more than 5,000 species of jumping spider worldwide. Two of their eight eyes, the median pair, are especially large and look directly forward, helping them judge accurate distances over a range of several centimetres. (It also makes them look rather cute!)

TOXIC BITE

Almost all spiders rely on venom for hunting: one quick bite and their dinner stops struggling! When a spider stabs its fangs into prey, powerful venom flows out through the hollow fangs, causing paralysis or death, so the spider can feed at leisure. The venom softens the victim's insides into a liquid 'soup', which the spider then sucks out. But first, of course, a spider has to catch its prey.

WOLF SPIDER
FAMILY LYCOSIDAE
Body size: 10–35 mm
(0.4–1.4 in)
Where found: Worldwide

FANGS
The woodlouse spider specializes in eating – can you guess? – woodlice (pill bugs). It has very strong fangs for piercing their exoskeleton.

VENOM
There are two main venom types. Neurotoxins attack the prey's nervous system and stop it moving. Cytotoxins dissolve the guts. Spiders may have one type or the other, or a mixture.

THROWING & SPITTING

First, weave your net...

The net-caster first spins frame-lines as a support structure. It then spins a small, net-like web onto its hind legs. The net silk is very stretchy.

Now, just hang around...

The spider now hangs downwards from its hind legs and holds the little 'net' in its front four legs, ready to pounce.

... now cast the net.

When a beetle walks into range, the spider stretches the net out by up to 10 times its original size, and casts it over the prey. The silk, spun using the spider's cribellum (see page 8), is made up of strands so crinkly and fine that the prey becomes completely entangled in it.

Well, that's charming.

The spitting spider squirts twin jets of silky venom from its fangs. Meanwhile, its body vibrates from side to side to create zigzag patterns in the silk, which glues the prey down like a sticky net. The attack is so fast (about three-hundredths of a second) that it can only be seen with a slow-motion camera.

AMBUSH PREDATORS

Net-casting spiders live in warm habitats from South America to Malaysia and Australia. They spin a little web that is just like a net, wait in ambush, then throw it down over a passing victim. They use their superb night vision – 12 times better than ours – to locate prey in darkness. Spitting spiders, which are more or less worldwide, squirt a mix of venom, glue and silk at their prey to pin it down.

NET-CASTING SPIDER
DEINOPIS RAVIDA

Body size: female up to 18 mm (0.7 in), male up to 14 mm (0.5 in approx.)
Where found:
Queensland, Australia

OGRES
Net-casting spiders are also called ogre-faced spiders. Their scientific name, *Deinopis*, means 'fearsome appearance'.

PERFECT AIM
The bolas spiders of Africa, America and Australasia spin a ball of sticky silk on a line, then swing it at flying moths to knock them out of the air.

BIG EYES
The large eye pair on an ogre-faced spider are the biggest simple eyes, relative to body size, of any arthropod.

FISHING

With a film of air around its abdomen, enabling it to breathe, the diving-bell spider spins a canopy of silk underwater, anchoring it to plant stems.

When the spider dives, a 'coat' of air clings to the hairs on its abdomen. The spider hauls its extra-buoyant body down with the help of silken lines.

The air bubble is held underwater in its silken canopy. Once it reaches a certain volume, the bubble 'fills' itself without further effort from the spider, because oxygen naturally filters into it from the water. This 'artificial gill' enables the spider to live underwater like a fish — and to hunt fish!

Dolomedes raft spiders have a coat of short, velvety hairs that repel water and help them float. Their sensitive feet detect the vibrations of moving prey, such as insects or small fish, which they catch at or below the surface. They can briefly dive, too, trapping a film of air around the abdomen.

WATERY HOME

How does an air-breathing creature spend its whole life underwater? The diving-bell spider, which lives in ponds and rivers, spins itself a silken dome beneath the surface, and fills it with air gathered from above. This oxygen tent becomes a home for the spider, which clambers out to hunt fish and other aquatic life. Raft spiders, too, can hunt on or below the surface, thanks to their amazing 'walk on water' skills.

DIVING-BELL SPIDER
ARGYRONETA AQUATICA
Size: 8–18 mm (0.3–0.7 in)
Where found:
Europe and Asia

UNDERWATER EGGS
Diving-bell spiders even lay eggs underwater. A few days after hatching, the spiderlings leave the nest to spin their own tiny diving bells.

BIG SPIDERS!
Raft spiders can be big, with leg spans as wide as the palm of your hand. Some have been known to catch goldfish!

CAMOUFLAGE

Matching its background perfectly, a crab spider is more or less invisible to its prey: insects that visit plants to collect nectar and pollen.

Like a commando in camouflage gear, the lichen spider is coloured and patterned just like a lichen-covered tree trunk.

Look very carefully near the tideline on American beaches and you may spot the seashore wolf spider – if you can see through its disguise.

The bird dropping spider – disguised as a splotch of poo – sneakily gives off a scent that moths find delicious. They visit... but don't leave!

Some of the most amazing camouflage is seen in tree-dwelling spiders, helping to hide them from birds during the day. Left: the wrap-around spider (*Dolophones*) is named after the way it flattens itself against a branch. Centre/right: at rest, twig spiders look just like stumpy little nubs of wood on a branch.

CLEVER CONCEALMENT

Spiders can be surprisingly hard to spot! Since most of them are sit-and-wait hunters, they have evolved very good camouflage. This not only conceals them from prey, improving their chances of catching a meal, but also helps hide them from predators such as birds. Spider camouflage includes amazing colours and patterns, and unusual body shapes, along with cryptic (hiding) behaviour.

GOLDENROD CRAB SPIDER
MISUMENA VATIA
Size: female 6–9 mm; male 3–4 mm
(0.25–0.4 in; 0.12–0.15 in)
Where found: All around
northern hemisphere

BLENDING IN
Usually found on yellow or white flowers, the goldenrod crab spider can change colour to suit its background.

SLOW CHANGE
It takes the spider about six days to change from yellow to white. Changing back takes four times longer, because the spider has to make new yellow pigment.

MIMICRY

This *Myrmecium* spider has the usual eight legs, but by waving its long front legs in the air just like antennae, it tricks ants into thinking it's one of them.

A ladybird's bright colours signal to birds that it is foul to eat. So it's no surprise that some spiders – like this *Paraplectana* – mimic the ladybird for protection.

Mimicry can go both ways. On the right is *Coccorchestes*, a jumping spider that mimics a bad-tasting weevil... while on the left is *Agelasta*, a longhorn beetle that mimics a crab spider! It's not clear why – but being a copycat must help the beetle in some way.

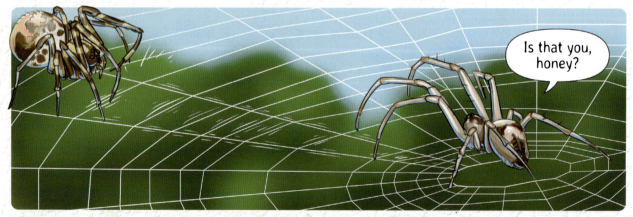

Ero cambridgei (left) is a pirate spider that preys on other spiders. Here, it taps the web of a female *Metellina segmentata* in a particular rhythm, to mimic the courtship signals of her mate. This will trick her into coming closer... right into Ero's ambush.

SPIDER TRICKERY

Many spiders have evolved to mimic (look, behave or even smell like) other creatures – such as ants, beetles or even other spiders. This trickery can enable the spider to get close to prey without raising the alarm. It can also give protection from predators, such as birds or spider-hunting wasps. For example, by looking like a bad-tasting beetle, a spider is less likely to be eaten.

ANT-MIMIC SPIDER
MYRMARACHNE MAXILLOSA
Size: female 6–7 mm (0.25 in);
male 5.5–8 mm (0.2–0.3 in)
Where found: Southeast Asia, southern China

ENEMIES
Stinging and biting ants are dangerous to spiders – especially when there's a 'gang' of them – so by mimicking an ant, a spider can evade attack.

DISCOVERY
It was English naturalist Henry Walter Bates (1825–92) who worked out that animals gained protection by mimicking others. He realized this from studying butterflies in the Amazon.

REPRODUCTION

Often the female is much bigger than the male. Just look at this pair of *Nephila* orb weavers. She, after all, will have the job of looking after the kids.

The male *Anyphaena* buzzing spider attracts the attention of a female by vibrating his abdomen noisily. It's a bit like ringing a bell!

To avoid being eaten, the male nursery web spider (left) may soothe a female (right) by offering her a gift of a chewed-up prey animal.

Some spiders wave their legs at each other in a complex 'sign language', to make sure they are ready to mate with one another.

Egg sacs may be buried, hidden, abandoned or guarded carefully, depending on species. Here, a raft spider carries her sac beneath her body, while a bird dropping spider has 'parked' hers on a twig.

FEMALES AND YOUNG

A female spider lays eggs, which hatch into spiderlings. These babies don't have the larval or pupal stages seen in most insects; they are true tiny spiders, and before long they are catching their own prey. Sounds easy? First, spiders need to mate, and it can be very dangerous for a male spider to approach a big, hungry female: she may decide to eat him!

WOLF SPIDER
FAMILY LYCOSIDAE
Body size: 10–35 mm
(0.4–1.4 in)
Where found: Worldwide

HITCH-HIKERS
The female wolf spider carries her egg sac on her abdomen. When the spiderlings hatch, they climb up onto her back and hitch a ride.

SILKEN TENT
The female nursery web spider makes a 'tent' of silk on a plant in which her babies can grow safely, while she stands guard outside.

SPIDERS & PEOPLE

The name 'tarantula' comes from this spider, *Lycosa tarantula*. Long ago, to cure its bite, peasants near Taranto in Italy performed a dance, the 'tarantella'.

In the 19th century, the black widow (*Latrodectus mactans*) – North America's most venomous spider – often built its web in outside toilets.

Carefully using a pipette, experts 'milk' venom from captive Sydney funnel-web spiders to make medications that can be used to treat spider bites.

Big hairy spiders, like this Mexican red-knee, make popular pets, but overcollection is endangering their populations in the wild.

A single spider can eat about 2,000 insects – flies, mosquitoes, aphids and so on – in a year. That's why many people put up with spiders in the home and do not squash them. So next time a spider builds its web in your house, give it room, and take a closer look...

THE DANGEROUS FEW

The strength of their venom, which can stop prey dead, unfortunately makes a small number of spiders a serious danger to humans. In most species, however, the fangs are just too small to puncture our skin. Also, modern antivenins (medicines) mean that bites are almost never fatal. Nevertheless, you should always treat spiders with respect. Better still, think of them as friends, as they help rid our homes of pests such as flies.

SYDNEY FUNNEL-WEB SPIDER,
ATRAX ROBUSTUS
Body size: 15–45 mm (0.6–1.77 in)
Where found:
New South Wales,
Australia

BEWARE!
About 12 cm (5 in) across, the Brazilian wandering spider is especially dangerous. It is highly aggressive and injects up to 8 mg of venom – enough to kill about 300 mice.

STRONG BITE
The Sydney funnel-web spider attacks again and again when disturbed. It bites so hard that its fangs can puncture fingernails.

Spiders & Their Enemies

The *Pepsis* tarantula hawk wasp is a huge wasp, up to 50 mm (2 in) long, with a stinger up to 7 mm (0.27 in) long. It specializes in hunting spiders.

Having paralysed a spider with its sting, *Pepsis* drags it back to its burrow in the ground. There, it lays a single egg on the spider and covers it over with soil.

When the wasp larva hatches, it eats the spider – beginning with the non-vital organs so that the spider is kept alive for as long as possible.

Mason and potter wasps also gather paralysed spiders for their larvae, storing them in cells built of mud.

The Australasian white-tailed spider (right) hunts at night... for other spiders. Its favourite prey is *Badumna*, a house spider.

With so many enemies, it's no wonder spiders are shy. Jumping spiders, for instance, often hide in a curled-up leaf by day.

A TOUGH LIFE

Being soft and plump, spiders make a nourishing snack for predators, ranging from birds and lizards to insects and even other spiders. Most fearsome of all are the wasps that sting spiders to paralyse them, then store them in a 'living larder' to feed to their larvae. There are flies, too, that burrow into a spider and lay eggs; the fly larvae later eat the living spider. The eight-legged life is tough!

BLACK-BACKED KINGFISHER
CEYX ERITHACA
Size: 13 cm (5 in)
Where found: India, Southeast Asia

SPIDER HUNTERS
Birds snatch spiders from their webs. They also use the silk as a soft lining for their nests. That's one reason why spiders like to hide during the day.

2D VS 3D
It's thought that, about 130 million years ago, spiders evolved 3D tangle webs from 2D orb webs. The more complex 3D webs were a better defence against wasps.

THE OTHER ARACHNIDS

Anything that runs around on eight legs, like the spiders, is classed as an arachnid. There are more than 100,000 named species in the class Arachnida and they include ticks, mites, harvestmen, scorpions, solifuges and whip scorpions, among others. As a group they are found all over the world, even in the oceans – and if you look closely, you can see some of them in your backyard.

Ticks are parasites, living on the skin of a host (such as you, or your dog, or a bird). Some are tiny; the biggest are nearly 2.5 cm (1 in) long. To find a host, many ticks wait with their legs outstretched at the tip of a grass stem. If you brush past them, they jump on. Then they bite into the skin and suck blood, swelling up as they do so. After feeding, they drop off and lay eggs in the ground.

Mites are found in every imaginable land habitat. Worldwide there are more than 50,000 species, feeding on dead plants, dead skin and hair, fresh blood… yuck! Most are too small to see – which is a good thing, because there could be hundreds of dust mites in your bed, right now. They might make you asthmatic or itchy, but otherwise they're harmless.

Harvestmen look a bit like spindly-legged spiders, but, unlike a spider, the two body sections are fused into one. Also, they have just one pair of eyes. They eat almost anything, from dung to plant material to animals alive or dead; unlike spiders, they can digest solid food. You might see a harvestman in sand dunes or heathland, walking jerkily on its thin legs.

Scorpions are found worldwide, with some 1,750 species. Most spend the day under a rock, hunting at night. They use the sharp claws on their palps to tear food apart. All use venom for catching prey, such as insects or mice, and for defence. The venom is injected from the *telson*, the final tail segment, which can be arched over during attack. Only 25 or so species can kill a human.

Solifuges, also known as camel spiders, sun spiders or wind scorpions, live in dry parts of the world. They hunt anything from beetles to lizards and rodents. Typically they have long, pointed jaws (which can make a chattering sound), and very long palps that resemble a fifth pair of legs. At up to 15 cm (6 in) long, solifuges look alarming, but pose little threat to humans.

Hello, eight-legged friends!

Whip scorpions include two groups. Amblypygids (above) live in warm places. They have a flattish body and eight long legs, although the first pair are used as antennae, not for walking. Vinegaroons look a bit like scorpions, but with a whip-like 'tail'. When disturbed, they can spray a sharp-smelling chemical, hence their name.

SIX SPIDER FACTS

The female desert spider *Stegodyphus lineatus* rears just one lot of spiderlings in her life, and literally dies for her babies. Her digestive juices soften the food in her stomach, which she then vomits up. Once the spiderlings have eaten that, they devour their mother, leaving just a dry empty husk. Then they leave the nest.

One of the most venomous North American spiders is the brown recluse or fiddleback, named after the violin-shaped markings on its abdomen. Its bite can kill young children, but luckily the spider is shy and attacks only reluctantly.

The six-eyed sand spider *Sicarius hahnii*, which lives in desert regions of South Africa, can go 12 months without food or water.

Really big mygalomorph spiders can kill and eat snakes – even 45-cm (18-in) rattlesnakes. They typically go for the snake behind the head, inflicting a fatal bite.

In parts of Cambodia, especially the town of Skuon, locals serve up crispy-fried spiders, each about as big as your hand. The taste, apparently, is halfway between chicken and fish!

The spiders in one family, the Uloboridae, have no venom fangs. Instead, they kill prey by wrapping it in very fuzzy silk – sometimes hundreds of metres of it – which eventually crushes the captive. Then they vomit digestive juices over the victim to soften it into an edible 'soup'.

GLOSSARY

abdomen   the hind part of a spider's body.

antennae   the two 'feelers' on an insect's head, providing touch, taste and smell. In some insect-mimicking spiders, the front legs look very like antennae.

Arachnida   the class containing the spiders and other eight-legged invertebrates. Members of the Arachnida are called arachnids.

cephalothorax   the 'head' part of a spider's body, made up of the cephalon (head) and thorax (mid part).

chelicerae   the two jaws either side of the spider's mouth. Each is tipped with a hollow fang.

cribellum   a comb-like organ beneath the abdomen, used for combing silk to make it woolly.

fang   the hollow, pointed part of a chelicera, used for biting into prey and injecting venom.

invertebrate   an animal without a backbone, such as spiders, insects and crustaceans

mimicry   copying the appearance, behaviour or some other feature of another animal.

mygalomorph   a primitive kind of spider in which fangs operate up and down, not in a pincer action. Mygalomorphs include the big hairy spiders that most people refer to as 'tarantulas'.

palps/pedipalps   a pair of organs, attached to the spider's head, which are used by a male to transfer sperm to a female. Palps are also used as feelers.

spinnerets   nozzle-like organs at the tip of a spider's abdomen, used for squeezing out lines of silk.

tarantula   the name belonging properly to the wolf spider *Lycosa tarantula*, but also used for any large hairy spider in the United States, or the huntsman in Australia.

telson   the tip of a scorpion's tail, holding the venom gland and stinger.

venom   poison that is injected (from a fang or a stinger) into prey.

Gotcha!

INDEX

The Author

British-born Matt Turner graduated from Loughborough College of Art in the 1980s, since which he has worked as a picture researcher, editor and writer. He has authored books on diverse topics including natural history, earth sciences and railways, as well as numerous articles for encyclopedias and partworks. He and his family currently live in Auckland, Aotearoa/New Zealand, where he volunteers for the local Coastguard unit and dabbles in painting.

The Artist

Born in Medellín, Colombia, Santiago Calle is an illustrator and animator trained at Edinburgh College of Art in the UK. He began his career as a teacher, which led him to deepen his studies in sequential art. Santiago founded his art studio Liberum Donum in Bogotá in 2006, partnering with his brother Juan. Since then, they have dedicated themselves to producing concept art, illustration, comic strip art and animation.

Picture Credits (abbreviations: t = top; b = bottom; c = centre; l = left; r = right)
© www.shutterstock.com:

1 cb, 2 cl, 4 c, 6 tl, 7 tl, 7 tr, 7 bl, 9 c, 13 c, 15 c, 17 c, 19 c, 21 c, 23 c, 25 c, 27 c, 28 tr, 28 cl, 28 br, 29 tl, 29 cr, 29 bl, 32 cr.

11 c © Bryce MQuillan NZ